# SURVIVING
## Peter Pan

*Let's see how far we fly* :)

### Poems
### Marissa Forbes

**Beyond The Veil Press**

Poems © 2023 Marissa Forbes
Cover Illustration © Claire Simpson
Manuscript © 2023 Beyond The Veil Press

All rights reserved. No part of this publication may be reproduced, distributed, or transmitted in any form or by any means, without the prior written permission from the author except in the case of brief quotations in articles and reviews.

Created on the lands of the Ute, Arapahoe, and Cheyenne peoples, in the so-called United States of America.

ISBN: 9798388001399

# TABLE OF CONTENTS

I. Preface by the Author     pg. 5-6
II. Poems
   *Chapter 1 - Shadows In Flight*     pg. 13
   The Luck Of A Kiss
   Wake to Dream
   Peter Triangulates Tinkerbell & Wendy
   Star Grazer
   The Last Night Before I Bleed
   Tink's Crime
   A Mother's Forest
   Wendy Cleans The Bathroom
   Being A Mother After You're Broken
   Roosters Vs. Fairies
   What Tinkerbell Thinks

   *Chapter 2 - We Stay Because We're Scared*     pg. 30
   Did We Come To Get Lost?
   Tiger Eyes, Lilies In The Sky
   Wendy Watches Peter Throw A Fit
   What A Never-Bird Does
   Peter Is Another...
   There's Power In No
   Which Wendy Will Survive?
   Don't Call Him A Forever Child
   To Be A Mother
   Playing House
   Hooked On, Hooked In
   The Mourning After
   Too Many Suns & Moons To Remember Mothers
   A Mermaid's Jealousy Will Drown Me
   For Which A Never-Adventure
   Neverland Comes From Stolen Gold
   What If Tiger Lily Drowned?

*Chapter 3 - The End Of Neverland*                pg. 54
Can I Pretend?
How Wendy Tells A Story
Does Cockiness Sleep Peacefully?
Pantoum For Peter's Pirate Father
The Next Generation
Men In Kennels
Returning To The Window
Box of Darkness
Freedom To & Freedom From
Healing Is Magic & It Is Not Magic
What Of The Lost Boys?
Cycles
Wendy's Daughter

III. Acknowledgements                                        pg. 73
IV. About The Author / About The Press          pg. 74-75
V. Bonus Content: Club Q Anthology Sample     pg. 77-86
VI. Other Titles By Beyond The Veil Press           pg. 89
VII. Mental Health Resources                          pg. 91

# PREFACE

My introduction to *Peter Pan* was around the age of five. My first *Peter Pan* was the 1960's Mary Martin when my Grandmother recorded the play off the TV and sent the VHS tape to my Mother. I was enamored with the entire production; you could say I was hooked on this reverse Shakespeare lady-in-tights playing a boy-man.

Martin had a joyful and gentle performance that convinced me Peter Pan was a good boy. A boy who just wanted to stay young forever and spread his love of all things adventurous. It wasn't until 30 years later that I would learn the dark magic of the boy who never wanted to grow up. Martin was a wonder who made me believe in dreams but a marriage to my very own Peter became my nightmare.

Throughout 2022 I was desperately trying to create anything that felt ordinary despite my incredible pain after my marriage imploded. I remembered the grasp *Peter Pan* had on me as a child, so I bought J.M. Barrie's novel, *Peter Pan* and began reading it to my kids. It was just my lost boys and me—their mother, who had long-gone lost myself too.

It was on the first page when I felt too much pain in, "Why can't you remain like this forever." I couldn't bring myself to continue reading the story to them with questions swirling: Why couldn't they stay my babies? Why couldn't our world remain as it was? Why was I so scared for this story to unfold for my two children? What didn't I want them to hear in those adventures pouring from the pages? I decided to absorb it alone before sharing it with them.

Then, I was pulled in…into a dark place. Through the gamut of narcissism, domestic abuse, coming of age with unhealed abandonment issues; along with the human urge to conquer and how that affects the ego, the story of *Peter Pan* is actually tragic. I couldn't help but read it through the scope of a girl becoming a mother with generational trauma. I took in this classic with fresh but pained eyes and felt the urge to flip the script of this narrative. When I finished the novel, I became dedicated to writing a survival story based on *Peter Pan.*

Even though it was an ugly, snot infested investigation of Peter Pan, this journey started at the right moment during my healing. I am a survivor and I can't write my experiences in a straight "I" yet so I use veils to convey my truth. I can't imagine a better metaphor than Peter Pan to expose my encounter with narcissistic trauma. Peter Pan is, after all, the most stunted male character in literature—he's the psychopath we all (think) we love. He became the maniacal lover I had to move through in order to move on from.

Peter also represents the harsh father-child relationship my children navigate. Whether Peter is just a fictional creature or my ex-husband, I acknowledge this collection is about me still learning to fly. Or, I'm learning to be grounded. Or, maybe, finally I'm finding the middle space after I have begun the journey back to the home inside my heart.

I took on the voices of Wendy, Tiger Lily, Tinkerbell, Neverland's mermaids, the Lost Boys, Hook, and his Pirates in order to see the trees and clouds, the stars and ships—the beauty through the pain. I feel better having *NOT* taken on Peter's voice in this collection because it is my mental health journey told in these pages. I explore Peter Pan's unabashed narcissistic abuse, Wendy's journey from girl to mother, Tinkerbell's rejection, Tiger Lily's burden, the terrifying connections between colonization and the body, generational cycles of trauma within families, and my own self-reflection.

This journey to Neverland is dark. It's told through a countering point of view than the usual story. It's a reclamation of a tale that's traditionally used as an excuse for men to infantilize themselves. But my poetry collection, *Surviving Peter Pan*, is a jumping off point for women and survivors of all ages and genders to give themselves grace.

*Surviving Peter Pan* is ultimately about my relationship with hurting and healing. This collection holds space for women as: lost girls, trying mothers, discarded lovers, strong warriors and sirens—of the Earth and sky, of the womb and heart. This recovery story is about me and my strength to see what I experienced isn't insanity. Neverland isn't a fantasy or a far-off place I put myself in as a form of denial, it's where I found my courage. It's a poetic story of strength, rather than just a fairy-tale of what Peter Pan wants us to be.

*Dedicated to Jack and Layne.
I hope you always have happy thoughts and wonderful adventures.*

# SURVIVING
*Peter Pan*

### *Poems*
### Marissa Forbes

*Beyond The Veil Press*

# Chapter 1
*Shadows In Flight*

# THE LUCK OF A KISS

A dinner date
begins with untied bow ties.
Grooming before goodbyes.
Forehead kisses. Winter mixes.

Then, slipping off a thimble.
Tiny metal ting-tings
across the floor when thread
pops through shadows.

Weaving needles—
sucking blood
bubbling at the tip
of the thumb.

Just put the kiss back in a drawer.
Don't pucker up.
I never-never
should have gone to Neverland.

## WAKE TO DREAM

I had a dream
    that a tiny bird
        flew into my room.
            Each time he hit a wall
                window, fan, or floor
                    he grew until I was carried away.

            A tickle on my palm.
         Stirred awake by kissable
      feathers. A young boy:
    his tiny chest
rising—falling
    as if he had been flying
        through his dreams.

        Or maybe mine.

# PETER TRIANGULATES TINKERBELL & WENDY

My untidy mind, on that flurry of a white night, with all that rushing around & fury when my Father—fragile like a porcelain vase—drugged our guard dog. But Peter knew. Took notice of the youngest lady in the manor. A lady aching for a mother. Or motherhood. Or just a lady who knew too little to know I needed to learn so much more.

There was a light on in the nursery. It burned hot until Peter said it was too dim for his shadow to shine. So, I put rose petals over my eyes, shielded myself under the duvet until the love-bombing rocked the bed frame. I sat up with a smile meant to be coy—no narcissist could resist.

Onward with forgetting what will be left behind. Tink in the drawer: banging fists in a square box filled with rage fit for a triangle. Did she know she was tied with a noose from the start? Peter pinned her against the largest lady she'd ever seen. I am just a giant fairy without wings.

Peter coaxed Tinkerbell—the tiniest of flickering beings, a light he shooed away with the flick of his hand—poor Tink forced to blow pixie dust on all the Darling children then guide our big bodies through the night. Furious Tinkerbell, the devalued little green garden lady, who maybe for a moment, wished she'd been forgotten in the drawer up in that nursery on the third floor.

## STAR GRAZER

I hold onto the sky, gripping white knuckled
drifting with the stars, dust smears over my skin
the moon oozes through my hands, light dripping.
Happy thoughts of the motherbed, curly hair & little toes
turning joys from sorrow, cloaking myself in bright patterns.
My spirit has wings, feathers sprouting on my boys, on brothers.
I watch them soar, spread love through mud
catching clouds with sticky fingers.

## THE LAST NIGHT BEFORE I BLEED

Disappearing wings made from the milky way
while rose buds bloom under my shirt.

Sleepy sweet tears streak into snot
freezing in my wind-blown hair.

& I'll forget
the drawer full of clean underwear.

Cradled between dolls & *boys will be boys*
skinned knees—all the same.

A body still void of stories.
In the morning, blood on the sheets
like a war without warning.

Sunbeams cascade through cumulus.
With my belly on a boat
& head in the bathroom—

whispering in the mirror:
> *Don't be scared of motherhood*
> > *or the absence of fathers*

## TINK'S CRIME

let's be honest
in the early breath of betrayal
anyone would call the other woman
a bird if she knew
a pack of boys dressed as animals
would shoot her down.

# A MOTHER'S FOREST

In the forest of how a mother can be:
I linger too long in far off places
twisted with tales—uneasy on my body.
Refracting light through leaves—
whispering into dirt.

A mother stands in the forest:
Grinding jowls, breathing deep
with fire through clenched teeth—
suffocating under the smoke
of bedtime stories.

In the forest of how a mother can be:
I wipe delicately, a child's face
with fingers wet with tears.
Hot porcelain doll cheeks—
all salty sorrows.

A mother stands in the forest:
Cradling ears in the crux of my arm—
heartbeats & crowing sync in the dark.
Can the gleam in my eyes ever flicker
on again?

In the forest of how a mother can be:
Leaves pile in the kitchen
mixed with flour & water.
Always sweeping myself
under the rug.

A mother stands in the forest:
Hair rolled with flowers & acorns—
mazes of color & no mirrors.
Every *I'm sorry* unravels
while plucking mushrooms off my skin.

In the forest of how a mother can be:
I mold red clay of the Earth
with blood under my fingernails—
rusty, dried, & angry.
Take a breath.

Step back & admire those lost boys
becoming their own warriors.

# WENDY CLEANS THE BATHROOM

I never-never would have come to this land
had I known I would gag
every time I placed little squares
of toilet paper on the seat to pee.

I never-never would have come to this land
had I known my nose hairs
would singe from the bleach smells.
My god, there's nothing worse
than trying to reach that spot
just below the toilet bowl,
on the outside of the base
were pee pools & dries.

I never-never would have come to this land
had I known I would get flakes of it
under my fingernails every time I scrubbed
that little yellow crusty puddle.

I never-never would have come to this land
had I known how terrible—how truly terrible—
fifteen lost boys are at aiming.
Peter is the worst of them all!
I've seen him through the crack in the door:
hands triumphantly on his hips
as he cock-a-doodle-do's
while pissing toward the porcelain bowl.

# BEING A MOTHER AFTER YOU'RE BROKEN

Peter has always been a rooster—screaming into the morning. The orange & yellow sky barely meets the tree line as steam swells in his throat. He flies back to the mermaids, back to the fairies, back to his tiger.

Lost boys lie on the floor outside my door. More than a hot brawl in my brain: suds between toes, pink skin up to my chin, pale knees like mountain peaks of aching questions. Peter laughs heartily when our boys grow drowsy in flight. We all fall from the sky—frightened with flailing limbs.

They've always been pirates—holding tightly to sea sickness & eye patches. Spying through the periscope, watching a burning candle just as it extinguishes. Peter baits alligators into my belly, coaxes crows to peck at my ears, sharpens swords on my spine.

Tinkerbell ties vengeance to my name. She cries in a thimble, sniffles through tiny tissues. Her light heart knows: *happiness actually comes when it's given to yourself*. Peter forgets. Or doesn't care—sipping on delusion like it's a sunrise & if he could, Peter would kiss his own feet. But why would he when he's got all of Neverland at his beckon call?

I've always been a mother—knowing it's more than a bedtime story, a peck on sore knees. More than pleading the same *please* again until it's just under breath. Grace comes after forgiving myself for putting Peter first because I'm no good when the wind blows me under the bush.

What if brothers never wake up? Always flying through slumberland, resisting the spiral all the way down the hill to the bottom of the forest. Forever picking up arrowheads—sharpened from stone & fear. But they don't want to fight for him. Never want to hold his feet, never want to crow the cock-a-doodle-doo of rage from their heart for him.

Together, against Peter. We whisper through R.E.M. cycles: *Please, please, please, think happy thoughts again.*

## ROOSTERS VS. FAIRIES

Broken beaks, dull claws.
I spent years plucking
my feathers so Peter could fly.

Hallowed bones breaking my skin.
I housed lilies inside
until I built his nest
& tried to call it my home.

Fed my body to the island
while he flew the coop.
Fed seeds to the lagoon
while he caught a swollen worm.

Peter returns south through snow.
I curl into tree roots
pulling arrows from my wings.

*Marissa Forbes*

## WHAT TINKERBELL THINKS ABOUT

If I could be anything else I would be:
                More than magic
                A fish
                Not a Neverland Native.

I don't exist to give birth
& death is a world without believing.
I'm lingering in between the flames.

        This magic takes away my mean.
        Being a fish is salt on my skin turning to scars.
        Maybe if I were more than stardust
        I would have a Grandmother.

What color will I become in my own fire?

    I've never found more than a marble
    but there are always seahorse clouds
    with saddles made of sunshine.

These words are not
about my pain or need for sunsets.
They're about you learning to clap your hands
& how I'll sink before I swim.

    Flying above the sea.
    The only word is *adventure*.
    Morning skies just give up
    so I catch a night vision.

        A pirate hooks me in his hand.
        We talk about constellations
        parlay & why we have long hair.

*Surviving Peter Pan*

    He wipes a tear from my eye
    with soot on his fingers.
    Then there's soot smears on my face.

Sometimes wings won't carry a resolution.
But my hair keeps growing
& I'll always have happy thoughts.

    I'll work on being forever.
    I'll learn to swim against the current.
    I'll hold the magic of feeling
    fear like an inferno.

# Chapter 2
*We Stay Because We're Scared*

## DID WE COME TO GET LOST?

*Peter never quite knew what twins were, and his band were not allowed to know anything he did not know. -J.M Barrie, pg. 60*

Idioms bite our brains
    like racoons in the dark.
We forget to abide.
    Disobedience hangs in the air—
        so, you leave us with blood
        on our clothes
        in our hair.

We stray from our dreams
    collect sticks clogging streams
        *stab each other in the back*
    & bring them to his feet.

"What about our mothers?"
    We ask over
    & over.
        Peter says, "It's over."

We come…
    & change our names.
His silence becomes that tiny space
        between rage
        or fear
        if there isn't any.
        *It takes two to tango.*

All that's left
is the mud crusted threats
never rinsed off our soiled feet.
        Soiled.

We come…
    & learn to crow for him, a language
        that washes over our tongues
        like dirty water.

*Surviving Peter Pan*

The bell on our Tink-Tink rings
& we hide under our bed
      where bent spoons rest
      with maps & slingshots.

We come...
      to be: sword fighters
            mushroom foragers
            firestarters.
                  *It's up in the air.*

Maybe we're here
because no one listened.
Maybe we're here
because luck is kelp
tied around our wrists.

We come...
      to be loved.
            We stay because we're
                      scared.

# TIGER EYES, LILIES IN THE SKY

I'm a Never-Earth Creator.
An Always-Cosmic Maker.
A vision on ethereal skin.

My invisible crown of yellowing ferns
& neon feathers
intertwine through raven hair.

Dirt streaks down my cheeks—
beautiful streams of mistakes
washing through the woods.

Paint on my skin cracks, colors fade.
Pigment stains my leather fringe.
Embers flicker on my lashes.

Silence in my skull—
ceramic Princess face
frozen with watchful eyes.

Yet, perpetual—ever so gently
climbing another tree to see below.
To protect from above.

## WENDY WATCHES PETER THROW A FIT

*Where do we close off our pain?*

    In our jaws, hands
        our shoulders?
            In our voice
                until it's gone?

*Go ahead, inhale.*
                Unclench & allow
            the pain to flow.

*Permission to soften.*
            It opens us
        to knowing.

*Exhale.*
            Softening loosens
    the masks
        we wear.

*Inhale.*
            Softening shows
           our bodies
              who we are.

*Exhale.*

# WHAT A NEVER-BIRD DOES

*"I-want-you-to-get-into-the-nest...then-you-can-drift-ashore, but-I-am-too-tired-to-bring-it-any-nearer-so-you-must-try-to-swim-to-it."*
-"The Never-Bird" Chapter 9, J.M. Barrie pg. 122.

She floats away.
Keeps floating away:
a paper boat gliding on the water's surface.
Sometimes a forgotten kite, lost in a tree.
Drifting to & from shore.
Heavy with wet wings. Exhausted.

>He's deserted on an odd rock
>cursing the black skies, hushing mermaids
>preparing his underwater dinner.

Sails cover the sun, destiny rising—
saltwater fingering his throbbing toes.

>He claps gayly toward the crashing waves—
>too daft to know a Never-Bird is meant to flap.

She floats with her soggy nest
toward his flightless boy-body. Drifting
with a desire to save someone's soul that day.

This Never-Bird floats to keep floating forward.
>Forgotten manners:

Demands & denials in different tongues—
reprimands & regrets at raging volumes.
>Call & response: Shut Up!
>*Shut up* isn't understood.
>*Shut up* anyway.

There's no stupid impetus
just stupid boys. Maybe stupid birds.
The wind carries: *Dunderheaded little Jay!*\*

Eggs are abandoned, her life returns to sky blue
with her future pulled from the nest.
      He winks at his own reflection on the shells…
          plopping them into their sea graves to meet the urchins.
The Never-Bird covers her eyes with drenched wings.

      He beaches the barque for the Never-Bird to find
but she keeps on. Never to touch ground
or water again.

---

*Pg. 113: Peter felt she was calling him names, and at a venture he retorted hotly: "So are you!"*

## PETER IS ANOTHER…

Colonizer:
    just a thief.

Great *White Stunted Man*:
    just a racist who speaks to shut you up.

Demander:
    just an ultimatum.

False *Father Knows Best*:
    just fingers over your mouth, a hand hovering your neck.

Time-Stopper:
    just another boy catching crocodiles.

## THERE'S POWER IN NO

I said *Yes* when you asked me to
be a mother, not knowing
you would make me feel guilty
every time I said *No*.

To have & to hold
never meant to fly & to cry
anytime you said:
*Because I want to...*

I need you to hear me.
Hear my *No* over
your cawing & crowing
your huffing & puffing.

You said the only role
of a Wendy
is to please her Peter.
& I threw up in my mouth.

Spewing *No*
all over the trees
dirt floor, moss
& splintered wooden door.

*No* became the ringing
in my ears.
*No* became the rising
sun in the sky.

*No* became the boys burning
at the bottom of the kindling.
*No* became your indent
on a cloud.

*No* replied to the fairy dust
on your breath.
*No* dug a deep hole
in our kiss.

*No* became another mermaid.
*No* became my dirty nightgown.
*No* became never again.
*No* became power & clapping hands.

I can never take back the *Yes*
but *No* gave me wings
to soar away.

Soar away
home, someday
on my own.

# WHICH WENDY WILL SURVIVE?

*Wendy in the bed*
    I know when he's near because the sound
    of his heartbeat.
    I see echoes inside his shadows.
    I ignore snowflakes dying on my duvet.

*Wendy in the sky*
    I know when he's here because the sound
    of his skin.
    I eat crumbs made of stars.
    I ignore the wind whispering *Go home*.

*Wendy in the woods*
    I know when he's around because the sound
    of his blood boiling.
    I smell rotten roots growing under my nightgown.
    I ignore the weight of being lost.

*Wendy on the ship*
    I know when he's close because the sound
    of time in his throat.
    I taste the burn of rope on my wrists.
    I ignore thimbles—pricking fingers as I sew his Captain's coat.

*Wendy at home*
    I know when he's *not* near because the sound
    of my own song.
    I don't leave the lights on.
    I ignore knocking on windows.

*Wendy as a real mother*
    I know when he's *not* around because the sound
    of my uterus swelling.
    I kiss (real kiss) the foreheads of my babies.
    I ignore the memories behind my eyelids.

*Wendy in age*
    I know when he's *not* here because the sound
    of my bones.
    I hold my palms tight. Then open, releasing the numb.
    I ignore *as it was*.

## DON'T CALL HIM A FOREVER CHILD

Let's not idolize his desires
nor forgive him his trespasses.
Just get him on the plank—
Can we skip the trial?
Let's not excuse his abuse
nor follow his footsteps.

## TO BE A MOTHER

is to be a kite, flying.
Flying until tilted off kilter.
Slipping down ribbons, hanging onto bows
tangled in branches made of limbs.

To be a mother
is to be tender.
Tender from bruises & near fractures.
Not of skin or bone
just my heart & mind.

To be tender & still wrap bandages
around boys playing limp
with unbroken arms resting in slings.

To be a mother:
tender & flying.
Sailing but frail.
To be flying
in & out of childhood.

# PLAYING HOUSE

in a tree, waiting for smoke to clear.
    But before it billows:

First, we must dance—
    no music, just fancy fascination.
The children beg
    until we sway by the fire.

I want him to be a real father.
    They're his and mine, after all.
He doesn't want to be old.
    Only make believe—that's his desire.

Greetings at the door are for ego
    slippers at his feet for guise.
Cock-a-doodle-doo doesn't make a Dad
    even though they look just like him.

Add a stick to the fire:
    Not even Tiger Lily wants to be his mother.
Another stick:
    Tinkerbell—the old supply, knows he's a silly ass.

Red flames engulf branches.
    The dancing stops with a snap.

## HOOKED ON, HOOKED IN

Endless cigar paper—a satin substitute
dressing his wounds.
Captain Hook traded his blood for steel.

Discomfort in dust coating tarnished billhooks
—in the tangle of whiskered cheeks & long fingernails.
Clocks & sun showers, even red feathers.

I fall into my strength to hear the seashells:
Loving the shore so hard
my humming tastes like crocodile skin.

I wonder about broken bones.
A slow, steady, shrinking, kind of thinking.
I wonder about his digested fingers.

       Tick-tock.
His hooks will rust unless I conjure up a second heart
to house our sweet pain.

Blinded by sunbeams.
Cracks in the periscope, light refracted.
       Ticking.

The strength of steel sinks down
to the brink of madness
at the lagoon's painted edge.

Not far from habit-forming insecurities.
       Tick-tock.
Commands carried in seafoam.

I pull the arrows from my back.
A small tear—ticking—splitting
where wings were meant to grow.

Near the end: oh dear! Stop looking back
at what our mothers might have been.

                        Tick-tock.

Swords clinking, blood on mermaids' hair.
We're all falling without fairy dust
without happy thoughts.

                        Tick-tock.

Crescent moons rise
—it's that damn crocodile here to harass—
pressing its grin between my palms.

                        Tick…

It's that damn Peter Pan
swooping in again.
Dragging me to the wind.

                        Tock.

# THE MOURNING AFTER
*For Wendy, Tiger Lily, & Tinkerbell*

Waking, restless
still orange glowing on skin
swollen from snot & slobber.
    Catching a lover in lies.

No more searing tears like snakes' venom
left in bones—broken & dried up.
Skin shrivels from sailing showers.
    Catching a lover in lies.

Screams soak into still water.
Drowning? Not yet.
Pale wrinkled bodies—cold.
    Catching a lover in lies.

Blurred vision, red-eyed.
This is what dying looks like
the morning after he killed us—
    Catching a lover in lies.

His faded, yellowing shadow
hiding in a drawer like a blanket
waiting for winter's freeze.
    Catching a lover in lies.

Not a fairy, mother, or woman warrior.
Just these sheets—
too taught for ever having held our body.
    Catching a lover in lies.

## TOO MANY SUNS & MOONS TO REMEMBER MOTHERS

In Neverland, there's no real day or night. Just too many suns & moons for time. Yet, that saying: *long days, short years* rings true every hour with too many suns & moons to remember Mothers. Real Mothers. The ones who swaddle newborns & meander through parks on brisk walks.

I collect tears & branches then scribe the color of my Mother's eyes on stones at the shore.
Slowly, I fill each rock with an answer:
> *Who was taller: Mother or Father?*
> *Was Mother blonde or brunette?*
> *What did her laugh sound like?*
> *How did she apply her lipstick?*

The Lost Boys follow behind, tossing each rock—each answer—out to the sea with spit wads. Bolstering laughter & snagging their socks along the way. The worst of it is, by the time I sit in my over-rooted home, rolling mended heels on my lap, I forget my answers.

Peter is eager to remind me that all my questions are in the past tense. Cackling with his adventurous matchsticks scraping across the bed frame. So boisterous as he lights the candle that flickers with my never-ending forgetting.

In Neverland, there's too many suns & moons for time. Long days. Short years. Another eternal hour. Too many suns & moons to remember Mothers. I'm not real. Not. A. Real. Mother.

## A MERMAID'S JEALOUSY WILL DROWN ME

Sirens in scales
& gills like heart valves—
open, shut them.
open, shut them.
Marooners Rock bakes in the midday sun.
Fins splish-splashing
briny water into my eyes.
A mermaid's laugh slices like fish bone
down my throat.
Her fury crashes like waves at the shore
as I dry on land—limp in the sand.
Seafoam bubbles leave salt on my skin
as the darkness comes.
There's a shiver in the sea
as if to say it has come.

As if to say it has come:
there's a shiver in the sea
as the darkness comes.
Seafoam bubbles leave salt on my skin
as I dry on land, limp. In the sand.
Her fury crashes. Like waves at the shore—
Down. My. Throat.
A mermaid's laugh slices like fish bone.
Briny water in my eyes.
Fins—splish splashing
Marooners Rock—bake in the midday sun.
Open-shut. Them.
Open, shut them:
& gills like heart valves.
Sirens in scales:
a mermaid's jealousy will drown me.

## FOR WHICH A NEVER-ADVENTURE

Adventure aches for pleasure.
Only it's fermented berries swirling in glass jars—
disturbances of the mind, body, & soul.

Adventure wakes the stars.
Only to swell in the sun—
feathers sprouting in the cap, tongue, & skin.

Adventure ticks like a clock.
Only out of rhythm, seconds inching toward worry—
off-beat without a heart, salt, & mothers.

Adventure opens the door to addiction.
Only it's never satiated—
hungry for higher, more, & never-ending.

## NEVERLAND COMES FROM STOLEN GOLD

*Contrapuntal—Read: 1. Left column 2. Right column 3. Across*

| | |
|---|---|
| From the first crack of a twig | a mother walking on eggshells |
| under foot. The colonizers echo | too scared to say No |
| offshore. Lost boys' arms outreached | to the man of the house. |
|     to Peter, as if the wind caught them by surprise. | |
| | |
|     Stout men, sharp as arrows | |
| curl limbs around branches. | Trauma runs through generations |
| With the cry of a coyote | then her boys' breath— |
| red rushes through bloodlines for decades. | Carries the stench of her yolk. |
| | |
|     What's another territory | |
| without a scheme to uproot? | Abandon in the morning light— |
| Unearth the nerves that register | Flying to his new bird, |
| iron twitching with the sunrise. | while mother fixes the nest. |
| | |
|     Peter & Hook's war over gold & age | |
| is just another game. | Denial is powerful. Who is the child? |
| Only this time without burlesque. | Shrinking from his delusion— |
| Real bodies, dead in the mud: | refusing to grow. |
| | |
| Native flowers burned | We took the fall in the faultiness, |
| for the sake of bees to be smoked out. | gave all the love we had to give. |
| Among the trees, moccasins bleed | We've ruptured more than our hearts. |
|     & below, the boys in honeycomb, sleep. | |
| | |
| Neverland comes from broken homes | No more fear in control, |
| where fantasies shelter the sun. | but we can save that love for ourselves. |
| Peter's cockiness led to coveting | We can crack the eggs— |
| & so he lost his boys & mother forever. | salted golden smiles, broken. |

# WHAT IF TIGER LILY DROWNED?

The moons wouldn't fall & fall & fall again on Neverland. Low tides abandoned. Our Native Princess's demise would flood the lands, trees bending under waves. Ships would splinter & rest on the ocean floor. Red like blood—the lagoon would bloom with algae. Mermaid scales would flake off & plant themselves into the undersoil—through nevertime, limestone forms. The distance between one adventure & another would shrink until it's scared of ending. The island would uncramp then spread itself too thin, like stars bursting just before morning.

Saving the great raven Tiger Lily from rope burns on her waist & a long swim with fish was Peter's greatest feat. Only he caught a dull delusion in his eye. Shoveled glory in his shoes & feasted on the skin of her kin. He dug heels deeper into the dirt. His long con: planting seeds in her belly & mind. He built his own scrawny army, stole gold & pixie dust. Then pissed on it. Pissed on it all.

Maybe it wasn't actually about Hook in the end, maybe Peter just cared more about his own reflection crowing back at him. Or maybe more about keeping an arbitrary feather in his hat. If Tiger Lily drowned, the two brooding bastards might have gotten over their Mommy issues. But Neverland would have fallen from the sky with Tiger Lily resting underwater. Twins would finally become two boys. Prams would roll back to their nurseries. Wendy would wake up with a thimble still on her thumb. Nana would break the door down & swallow shadows.

But Tiger Lily didn't drown & Neverland remains threatened.

# Chapter 3
## *The End of Neverland*

## CAN I PRETEND?

I can pretend, but chivalry doesn't impress me.

To a fault, I might be wooed by the slight of hand that helps steady my feet—if only to lead me to my boys—tied up like turkeys ready for the fire. Entranced over & over & over again. Until the crying is drowned out by singing. Tone deaf & wailing. False drums coax us. The last boy from my pretend life—the one who never stopped pretending—reaches out in the darkness with his periwinkle eyes.

I can pretend, but I welcome the break from my songs & bedtime stories.

Those songs that lull them boys to sleep. But no matter how tired I am, Peter is the sleeping creature—snoozing on the great bed while the enemy slips into the abode. While the flame forgets what an ember feels like. While the land becomes less...until never.

*Who's alone now?*

I can pretend, but I still ache from this tragedy.

The tragedy of ropes & night-time pirates. As I secretly swear my gratitude, Peter plays his pipes to prove he doesn't care. Peter skips my medicine & doubles the poison. Peter vexes me as if I'm the one pouring tears out of his head. As if I'm the one seeping nightmares into his slumber when his arms—pricked with needles—hang from the edge of the bed.

I can pretend, but I'm done.

I'm gone. Never again for Peter to lie upon & cry. To wiggle calmness from my breath as he lets his devilish laugh melt from his mouth like a long-burning beeswax candle. Peter's anger toward me is *really* him riddled by his own existence. Neverland's unspeakable crime is really his to carry: moons shining through all the leaves of the forest—dripping with blood.

I can pretend, but I still hold in my screams.

Breath collecting in my lungs, slowly escaping like the cosmic sounds only visible to the stars. Kidnapped, yet again—only this time from toxic promises echoing in the winter sky. Is it still winter where I'm from? Peter is defenseless. It was bound to happen sooner or later.

I can pretend, but Hook found him.

Peter's got no necks to wring. No fairy dust to throw, or fish scales to scrape off. Poor Peter has no one to tell him how much they need him. No one to tell him when summer will come. Peter's self-indulgence is so grand he can only hear the drums for victory—too self-righteous to know they're tricks. He's just living in the space between dreams & waking now.

I can pretend, but I'll never be a little girl again.

*At least I'm not scared to be alone.*

## HOW WENDY TELLS A STORY
*Erasure from Chapter 11: "Wendy's Story" J. M. Barrie, p.126-129*

Listen then.
There was once a gentleman.

Quiet.
There was also a lady.

She is not dead.
Oh, no.

Oh, dear.
They were married.

No.
Quiet.

Oh, dear. Oh, dear.
All the children flew away.

They flew away
to Neverland

where the lost children are.
Hush. Now,

consider the feelings
of the unhappy parents

with all their children flown away.
Think of the empty beds!

If you knew how great is a mother's love
you would have no fear.

The mother would always leave
the window open.

So, they stayed away for years
and had a lovely time.

See, dear brothers.
(*Sshhh*).

There is the window standing open.
Over which we draw a veil.

## DOES COCKINESS SLEEP PEACEFULLY?

You are most vulnerable in slumber
with your mouth dribbling slobber—
welcoming evil to sit on your teeth.

Only children beseech a single light to remain on
but that's where shadows live—
where your eyes suspend just before dreamscapes enter.

You're the type to catch forty winks where you fall
so, surely the rattle of a door in the real world mixes
into your ego-driven sleeping visions.

The pain on both sides of your eyelids
clashes like twin energy levels.
So, your head shatters on the feather pillow.

You don't believe in the power of a good mattress
because self-blame never wrinkles your sheets.
Never ticks with alarm clocks or smears your war paint.

Tonight, there's a hand hovering over your face
or, could it finally be your own shadow, haunting?
No. It's redemption in the shape of a hook.

Maybe Captain Hook isn't a nightmare.
Is it evil to kill the boy who stole Neverland
& ruined the hearts of all the inhabitants?

No. He's a hero
because your dreams flip reality with the rip
of steel through a bed sheet.

But still you sleep.
Thrilled, with your hand gripped
on a dagger. Like a true Narc Pan.

## PANTOUM FOR PETER'S PIRATE FATHER


All this talk about mothers & we've forgotten damaged fathers.
Rage is the only claw sharper than an iron decree.
Scratch that, maybe it's envy that plucks roosters free of feathers.
Pirates & Peter living in a spiral of cycles, both too scared to break free.

Rage. Is the only claw sharper than an iron decree
Hook? Is the only father-figure Neverland children smile upon
Pirates or Peter? Living in a spiral of cycles. Both too scared to break free.
Some play while others die at dawn.

Hook is the only father-figure Neverland children smile upon.
Are Pirates just stow-away Dads looking for lost boys?
Some play. While others die. At dawn
the second star to the right is a dream catching fire as it destroys.

Are Pirates just stow-away Dads? Looking for lost boys—
scratch that. Maybe it's envy that plucks roosters free of feathers.
Sharpening their own stunted growth, cutting throats with knife toys.
All this talk about mothers. & we've forgotten damaged fathers.

# THE NEXT GENERATION

> *Some of them wanted it to be an honest ship and others were in favour of keeping it a pirate; but the captain treated them as dogs, and they dared not express their wishes to him even in a round robin. Instant obedience was the only safe thing.* -J.M. Barrie, p. 181

Us Lost Boys cry in our sleep after death swells our fingers.
There's a sharp clink-clank of swords in the wind:
*poor form* echoes through the clouds. *Poor form.*

First, we blind the grown men with lanterns.
Can't count past seventeen so we reckon that's the tally
of each stab—good in the gut until they're all dead.

Forced to strangle our desires for love
in our bare dirty hands. Only then can we take flight
with the black sails at full mast.

We must kill off the precious parts of ourselves
with secret raucous & cock-a-doodle-doos
until the pirates find their long rest with Davy Jones.

We've still got our mother until Thursday
so the pirate's waistcoats & trousers will be mended.
Snipped & sewn to fit our tiny frames.

By morning, we're chewing tobacco
& mopping decks, singing *Hi-ho-ho-hum*
with Captain Pan calculating the next mis-adventure.

He barks orders—nothing new. We're bigger dogs now
with a sting in our growing bones.
Waiting for that blade to cut whiskers from our faces.

## MEN IN KENNELS

Oh, here's a metaphor: A father's anger swells until his children run (rather fly away) to as far as *never again*. I mean Neverland. And then, instead of saying, "I'm sorry," he just climbs into a kennel and locks the door.

My oh my! Another metaphor: The great heart of the collective is touched. Suddenly the father is celebrated. Yes, that's right, his excessive pity puts him on a pedestal. With a small procession following the father in his kennel to and from work, he says, "Listen to them…it's very satisfying."

Poor Mother, with her tired eyes. Even she can see he's enjoying his self-inflicted punishment a bit too much. Oh my, yes, another metaphor.

## RETURNING TO THE WINDOW
### Extended Katuata on Manipulation

All you need to know:
their Mother left the window
open but Peter snuck in.

He barred and locked it.
Glee from Wendy's misery:
*then she will come back to me.*

## BOX OF DARKNESS

My box of darkness lived under my bed through another cold winter. Locked up with his secret shadow seeping out—becoming a ghost trying to haunt the blood blooming in me. Fire in my gut, having just begun to sync with the moon. Monthly rage rips through the sky like a comet. An echo ringing in my ears late at night.

After stuffing bedtime stories into my pockets, delicately, I pull the box closer to my chest. Digging fingers—crescents on my palms—and thumbing my future in a hollowed coffer. Why doesn't anyone ever tell a girl she doesn't have to grow up?

Snow thaws because a girl becomes a woman before dawn breaks. Before she is asked to give up her own dreams. Before blood gushes, before water rushes. The skies part for the future as memories sleep on my skin. The sun aches to dry dew drops on my eyelids.

My box rattles under my pillow. It splinters as I crack it open at the seams with a broken key. Peter's shadow rises. Instead of sewing it back on, my fingers wait. He's carried and laid to rest in a field of poison ivy. My box of darkness is shallow without adventure.

I pulled moss from my underwear. Planted, watered, and nurtured my own sorrow seeds. I grew up without the need to pretend. In the soft warmth of Spring, daffodils sprout from the dirt, lavender plucked for my tea in the Summer eves. My box of darkness became a garden.

## FREEDOM *TO* & FREEDOM *FROM*

are tricks that stick
to my ribs & sit just below my heart.

Freedom *to* choose for myself
–restricted–
no more open windows.

Trees hidden by roots, overgrown.
Will I ever have a bed of my own again?

Freedom *from* capture is a falsity
–violence–
drop your dreams in the dust.
Broken toy swords & bullet-proof turtles.

Neverland is a loopty-loop
trapping all the babies I carry & grow
& carry some more.
They're forced to act it all out.

What about little mother birds?
What about tears & terrible fathers?

The forest sons don't know how to separate
yesterday's lies against tomorrow's hope.

Is Freedom *to* & Freedom *from*
just an everyday play-battle turned massacre?
It's 365 days a year (or maybe doubled
times three, no one can tell).

I feel the real beat—
the space between fear & earaches.
Except, an endless day…all over again.

Can wombs that carry & grow ever rot?
Can they learn to birth justice again?

Not if magic doesn't get off my body.

# HEALING IS MAGIC AND IT IS NOT MAGIC

Can there be magic, only hiding?
We tie whistles to our names.
Marching in skin shedding streams of static sounds.

I'm just a girl, among the abandoned many
flapping arms all about—
avoiding all the forever-boys' elbows.

Brothers aren't born as loud songs
through broken trumpets.
Healing is starving those deafening thoughts.

Sisters fester like needles & thread
stuffed into knotted balls of yarn.
Healing is wrapping yourself in mended socks.

Fathers age like whittled pieces of bone.
They don't ask to splinter.
Healing is letting the meat rot.

Mothers are nestled screams in jars—
they can't help but hold onto loss.
Healing is taking the lid off.

Husbands & wives sleep like ships in the night;
floating apart in rough currents of contrition.
Healing is making the bed.

Not everyone needs someone.
I know because we are strangers now.
I'll take blame for the honeybees.

But you crushed them all under your bare feet.
Healing is extinguishing the match
that lights every sting on fire.

Forget about alchemy.
You burned the imaginary oven to rust.
Healing is scraping the scorched crust.

My tired blood & nerves rest outside my body—
Sunken down with soggy nightgowns & daydreams.
Healing is living & retelling the same adventures.

Too many trees were cut down:
fields filled with broken families & charred stumps.
Healing is sowing new seeds.

I went to bed broken, woke up unwoven.
There is no resolution—no band of women. Just boys, lost.
Healing is a honeycomb in my hair.

We never became shadows—*they're not real.*
We become our defenses instead.
Healing is untying the whistles.

# WHAT OF THE LOST BOYS?

As with all boys, they grew up.
But fear for a Mother is in sleepless nights:

> *Are they kind?*
> *Do they listen to "No"?*
> *Are they always angry?*
> *Do they say, "I'm sorry"?*

You will see them sit in cubicles
like they're sliding down a tree.

> *Are they smart?*
> *Do they listen to "Please"?*

You will see them carry an umbrella
like they'll catch flight in the wind.

> *Are they ambitious?*
> *Do they have a gentle touch?*

Always in their mind's eye:
A stick is a sword.

> *What if?*

A rock is a cookie.

> *Why?*

A girl is always a Mother.

> *No.*

There are always…
traces of fairy dust in their blood.

There are always…
clouds in their ears.

> *For a mother*
> *there are always…worries.*

# CYCLES

Mothers & sons. Fathers & daughters.
There are specks of ivy in all our eyes.
Some fathers can't hold a flame to anything but lies.
False promises for safe adventures.
Only to claim he never said "safe."
Hen & hornet. Rooster & egg.
Either way, nests are abandoned.
Pan learned to fly so he wouldn't have to run.
False skills for his own fear.
Only to claim he's never been scared.
Husbands & wives. Lovers & others.
Hearts beat in the cracks of broken branches.
Cycles call for the return year after year.
After.
Year.

# WENDY'S DAUGHTER

I leave Wendy here. *I don't have a daughter.*

I join the Mother's movement to stop years rolling on & on & on with more sons forgetting all their hurt. All that hurt their Peter caused. Their Captain Pan with dead eyes & a hallowed heart.

Even though she remarried, Peter is her first husband & all the lost boys are her first children.

My place in real life is to survive my own Peter Pan & to give my real babies a lasting taste of the good parts of Neverland. To teach them how to leave evil out of their DNA.

Mothers can't help but tell their stories. Otherwise, they fill their minds with questions & concerns for their children. Days full of tears & I'm sorry. Nights full of tears & I'm still sorry. If they don't tell their adventures they'll lose them. Forever.

Wendy planted that sick sad seed of false love in her daughter. Told her all the grand parts: the flight & stars, the mermaids & fairies. Wendy left out the falling & mud, the biting-your-tongue, & crying to sleep.

As for me, I've got to teach my boys about splinters, about how they've got to catch people when they fall. Not laugh as they land.

I've got to teach them how to sew on their own shadows because they can't take the credit when a woman does it. I'll let them know I won't stand for them stealing thimbles. Let alone a kiss.

I've got to teach them to remember their past. Teach them to tell the truth. To say, "Thank you."

If I had a daughter, I would have taught her to never do a man's Spring cleaning, never be convinced that it's okay to steal another woman's man. Whether she is a fairy or not.

I would have taught her to never let her feet get too far off the ground. Never follow someone else's adventures—I would have taught her to make her own.

I would have told her Tinkerbell's story, Tiger Lily's story. I would have learned the names of every mermaid and told their stories.

But, Wendy's daughter asked, "Boy, why are you crying?" & now the cycle of flying through Peter's Neverland continues for her daughters. & her daughters' daughters...until maybe some night, in a Neverland future, a Darling daughter doesn't ask Peter why he cries.

Until that night comes when a Darling daughter sees her Peter is only crying to capture another false mother. I can try to teach my boys how not to become another Peter.

# ACKNOWLEDGEMENTS

*Versions of the following poems have appeared in publications:*

*Healing is Radical & It Is Not Radical* Musing Publications, 10.2022.

*The Last Night Before I Bleed* South Broadway Ghost Society Online Lit. Journal, 01.2023.

Portions of the poems have appeared on my Instagram: *@word_nerd_ris*

The novel, *Peter Pan* by J.M. Barrie is public domain.

## ABOUT THE AUTHOR

Marissa Forbes (she/her) is an artist, writer of all genres, instructor, and mother. She has self-published a limited-edition poetry chapbook called My Muse Is a Night Owl and her full length collection Bridging the Gap: Poems & Ethos for Emily Warren Roebling is forthcoming from Finishing Line Press in the fall of 2023.

She is the Managing Editor for Twenty Bellows, a Colorado based literary magazine with a mission to amplify marginalized voices of the west. She also teaches the National class for a 10-month poetry publishing program through Community Literature Initiative. Forbes was awarded an Author Fellowship from Martha's Vineyard Institute of Creative Writing in 2021 and is a Pushcart Nominee for 2023.

She has resided all over the country but found her forever home in Denver where she lives a colorful life with her two children, Jack and Layne, a dog, and cat.

Her published poems and stories can be found on *marissaforbes.com*.

## ABOUT BEYOND THE VEIL PRESS

Beyond The Veil Press is a queer-owned indie publisher based in Colorado.

We began as a Kickstarter project by two SCAD graduates (Sarah Herrin & Josiah Callaway) in March 2021, with a goal to promote the healing power of poetry & art while lifting the veil from "scary" topics of mental health.

Since then, our small team of volunteers has grown to include AJ Wojtalik, Tyler Hurula, Kris Kaila, most recently Salem Paige. (Visit our site to meet them!) We believe that by sharing our darkest stories, we find we are not alone.

We donate 10% of each anthology sale to a featured mental health nonprofit. Please see our mental health resources page on our website and on the following page.

*beyondtheveilpress.com*
*IG: @beyondtheveilpress*
*FB: /beyondtheveilpress*
*Twt: @MrBiteyBTVPress*

*Sample*

# *We Apologize For The Inconvenience*

## *Club Q Benefit Issue*
## *Queer & Trans Voices*
CW: mentions of death, suicide, and grief

Poetry & Art
**Beyond The Veil Press**

## CLUB Q NEWS IN THE OTHER ROOM
*Angel Leal*

I'm asleep, swimming in a blue dream.
My partner, trembling in the other room,
didn't wake me. They let me stay
in a watery ignorance. When I crawled
out of sleep, they smiled, lifted me
like a pile of sand dollars. Gave me time
to collect myself before I found their
death. Now I'm awake, my love. Thank you
for letting me swim a little longer.

*We Apologize For The Inconvenience*

**QUEER CRASH**
Mixed media collage
*Duna Haller*

# ALL QUEER SUICIDES GO TO HEAVEN
*Emily Long*

& the Pulse victims are there, too,
& Audre & Sappho & Alvin & Marsha & Sylvia
& the missing generation of elders lesioned
by a government who made them a punchline.

Of course all queer ancestors go to heaven. But
so do the ones who are their own crumbling
& wrecking ball, take their lives
into their hands by taking them away.

The ones who have wrestled the knife
from their attacker's fist only to house it in the dependable
home of their own body, who have flung open
every cobwebbed closet looking for a reminder

they're not already a ghost. We're the
ones who never found safety anywhere
but the trigger of a gun. We're bathroom stall lunches,
alleyways not quite home, revolving doors & changing locks.

We're bruises blossoming from sticks & stones,
yes, but the autopsy alleges internal bleeding is the cause
of death, glass shard words implanted & infected. We amputate
the whole body to save a sliver of self still clean.

We're my best friend who received
so many death threats by the age of 20
she decided to just do it herself.

So yes, we get our own Elysium, & here, we heal
in all shades of *tell me where it hurts*.
I tell you who I am & that's who I am.
There is no need for the word *trauma*;

to break is to kaleidoscope, to swing
dance with tender light. Wounds
bloom into buds into gardens,
all perennials.

Why must paradise always be an afterlife?

I'm an atheist but I have to believe in something
softer for her, for us. & I cannot believe
too zealous because then I will be swimming after them,
enough coins sinking my pockets to pay Charon's toll.

& yet. Here we are, planting lavender
in our scars & it's not young soil on a grave.
Most days I'm not sure how to stay
when so many could not but maybe

that's beside the point.
A closet is just a closet.

You don't need to come out,
you just need to come home.

## STEPPING INTO QUEER GRIEF
*Susan Niemi*

Michelle Abdill and Roxanne Ellis - the first
Victims' names I spoke in remembrance
And in protest of their execution for being
Lesbians - 12-4-1995, Medford, Oregan.

A candlelight vigil and protest were held by
The San Diego Lesbian Avengers, I was
A new member after coming out publicly.
Collective mourning - was my first action.

Suddenly I was waist-high in my new
Community's grief and rage at the loss
Of two strangers turned sisters - family.
The fear and hate are directed at us all.

Silently I wrestle between stepping back
Into the closet or avoiding the places where
I might become victim - my insides tremble
When I consider leaving the safety of home.

Michelle and Roxanne left Colorado Springs,
Colorado, 5 years prior to death, due to rising
Homophobia to continue fighting for gay rights.
Too many names join theirs to those lost to hate.

Queer grief spends little time bargaining
To undo death – we are too busy planning
Memorials, protests, and political actions to
Prevent the next attack we know will happen.

11-20-2022 we woke to the news of the attack
On Club-Q, safe haven for Colorado Springs
LGBTQ+ community - a place of celebration.
We lost the following queer siblings that night.

Daniel D. Aston (he/him) – Kelly Loving (she/her)
Derrick Rump (he/him) – Ashley Paugh (she/her)
Raymond G. Vance (he/him). We say your names.
Rest in Power - You Are Loved – Remembered.

**LET BOYS BE TENDER**
Illustration and digital
*Justin Demeter*

## TO EVERYONE WHO IS MY LIFELINE, EVEN IF I DIDN'T TELL YOU ABOUT IT
*Leona Boomsma*

It is hard to recover when you have seen
your own death played in front of you
more than a few times.

When you become so obsessed with
death that you've already picked
the flowers that should be

growing on your grave. I want them
to be colorful like a rainbow
so that you can find a cheerfulness

that I was lacking. When you feel
lonelier than you have ever felt
before. Heavier. Empty. Numb.

Then I will be thinking about you,
my loved ones, the reason I want to
keep trying. You are my lifeline,

and trust me, I'm holding on

so damn strong.

*We Apologize For The Inconvenience*

MY VOICE
Mixed Media Collage
*Angie Ebba*

# OTHER TITLES BY BEYOND THE VEIL PRESS

**2023 - Coming Soon!**

Anthology 6: LGBTQ+ Pride
Chapbook Contest Series featuring: Teddy Goetz, Ashley Mezzano, Jess Cato, and Kyrsta Morehouse.
Anthology 7: TBD
Neurotica For The Modern Doomscroller by Eddie Brophy

**2023**

Anthology 4: We Apologize For The Inconvenience - Queer & Trans Voices (Club Q Benefit Issue)
Maybe She's Born With It, Maybe It's Trauma! by Cait Thomson
Anthology 5: Identity

**2022**

Anthology 2: Tea With My Monster
Heretic: A Story of Spiritual Liberation in Poems by Kristy Webster
Anti/Muse Adult Coloring Book
Anti/Muse Lined Notebooks
Anthology 3: How To Heal A Bloodline

**2021**

Anthology 1: There Is A Monster Inside That I Am Learning To Love
Anti/Muse: Poems by Sarah Herrin & Illustrations by Josiah Callaway

*All books are (or will be) available in paperback and ebooks.*

# MENTAL HEALTH RESOURCES we love

*DIAL 988 IN A CRISIS*
*We are artists - not medical professionals. Please seek professional help if you are in crisis.*

## BOOKS

*Permission to come home: reclaiming mental health as Asian Americans* - Jenny Wang
*The Pain We Carry: Healing from C-PTSD for People of Color* - Natalie Gutierrez
*Journey Through Trauma* - Gretchen Schmelzer
*The Deepest Well* - Dr. Nadine Burke Harris
*My Grandmother's Hands* - Resmaa Menakem *tw: police violence
*What My Bones Know* - Stephanie Foo
*The Journey From Abandonment To Healing* – Susan Anderson
*Waking The Tiger* - Peter Levine
*Polysecure: Attachment, Trauma, & Consensual Nonmonogamy* – Jessica Fern
*Self-Therapy: A Step-By-Step Guide to Healing Your Inner Child Using IFS* - Jay Early
*The Body Keeps The Score* – Bessel van der Kolk *problematic but worth reading

## WEBSITES

activeminds.org - Mental health awareness and education for students.
afsp.org - Saving lives and bringing hope to those affected by suicide.
adaa.org - Anxiety & Depression Society of America
thetrevorproject.org - Crisis intervention and suicide prevention services for LGBTQ+ youth.
RAINN.org - for survivors of sexual assault

## PODCASTS

Where Is My Mind? – Niall Breslin
The Hilarious World of Depression; Depreche Mode – John Moe
The Happiness Lab – Dr. Laurie Santos
Speaking of Psychology – Kim I. Mills
Being Well – Dr. Rick Hanson and Forrest Hanson

## APPS

Headspace: Meditation and Sleep Made Simple
I Am Sober

**THANK YOU FOR SUPPORTING SMALL BUSINESS!**

Made in the USA
Monee, IL
21 May 2023